I Meet Myself Return

Photo by Denise Roberts

John Darwin thought he was a poet from birth, but was kicked into action by his Dad's terminal illness and a desire to do something more than shifting papers and supping pints. For two years, he was the host of Write Out Loud Sale, a member of A Firm of Poets for a couple more, and is co-host at Spoken Weird, Halifax. He lives, drinks, loves and laughs in Prestwich, North Manchester.

Also by the author

Misery Begins at Home
[Rubberybubberyboy Parchment, 2010]

Holding Your Hand Through Hard Times
with *A Firm of Poets*
[Ossett Observer Presents, 2014]

The People's Republic of Poetry
with *A Firm of Poets*
[Ossett Observer Presents, 2015]

I Meet Myself Returning

John Darwin

Flapjack Press
www.flapjackpress.co.uk

Exploring the synergy between performance and the page

Published in 2019 by Flapjack Press
Salford, Gtr Manchester
www.flapjackpress.co.uk

ISBN 978-1-9996707-5-7

Twitter: @DarwinPoet

Cover design by Brink
www.paulneads.co.uk

Printed by Imprint Digital
Upton Pyne, Exeter, Devon
imprintdigital.com

Dedicated to Andrew Watkins
1966-2018

Contents

Introduction 9

Happy New Year 13
Pearl diving 14
Number 22 15
Nordic Hotel, Leeds 6 16
Skipper 17
Thirteen Franciscans 18
And not a word of Spanish 19
Stanley 20
The sadness of strangers just passing 21
Strings 22
Icicles 23
Spring in Heywood 24
Football and girls 25
New school blues 26
Melanie 27
He's whistling Sinatra 28
Ffynon Farm 29
Mr Wilson said 30
Twenty 31
Palace of shyness 32
The transparent truth of Scientology 33
At four o'clock 34
Fifty-five winters 35
September 36
Islands 38
Where there's a will 39
Carp fishing in Shropshire 40
Seven hills 41
The tissue seller 42

After Orhan Veli Kanık 43
Death by drunken fall 44
Dawn in Galata 45
Dreaming in Turkish 46
Balm 47
Rascal 48
Manchester, my winter 49
Dreich 51
I meet myself returning 52
The ale glass 53
Listening to Sinatra 54

'Stanley' was first published in *The People's Republic of Poetry* [Ossett Observer Presents, 2015].
'The tissue seller' and 'Rascal' were first published in *Holding Your Hand Through Hard Times* [Ossett Observer Presents, 2014].

Introduction

This is a book about location, feeling at home.
I am no globetrotter, I got on a plane for the first time when I was 31.

It's about feeling homesick when you don't know where home is.

My permanent home is in Manchester.
I have lived there for 28 years, although it felt like home for many years before, through football and music.

I have felt at home as a very young lad in St Albans, Hertfordshire, where I was born...
In West Wales on childhood family holidays...
In Yorkshire where I grew up.

Brief moments of joy in the arms of a loving family, despite an unhappy education and suffering Leeds United winning trophies (well, two) whilst my club struggled and failed.

It's about finding a foreign culture which made me welcome and feeling loved...
In Turkey, the streets, bars and bridges of Istanbul are my second home.

It's about the joy of lazy summers with loved ones on the coast.

It's about the accumulation of wealth, acquisition, the constant striving for more things; the things which make us sad.

This collection is for every person I have ever loved.

You know who you are.

John Darwin
December 2018

With special thanks to
Geneviève L. Walsh, Dominic Berry,
Steve O'Connor, Angela Topping
and Brett Evans.

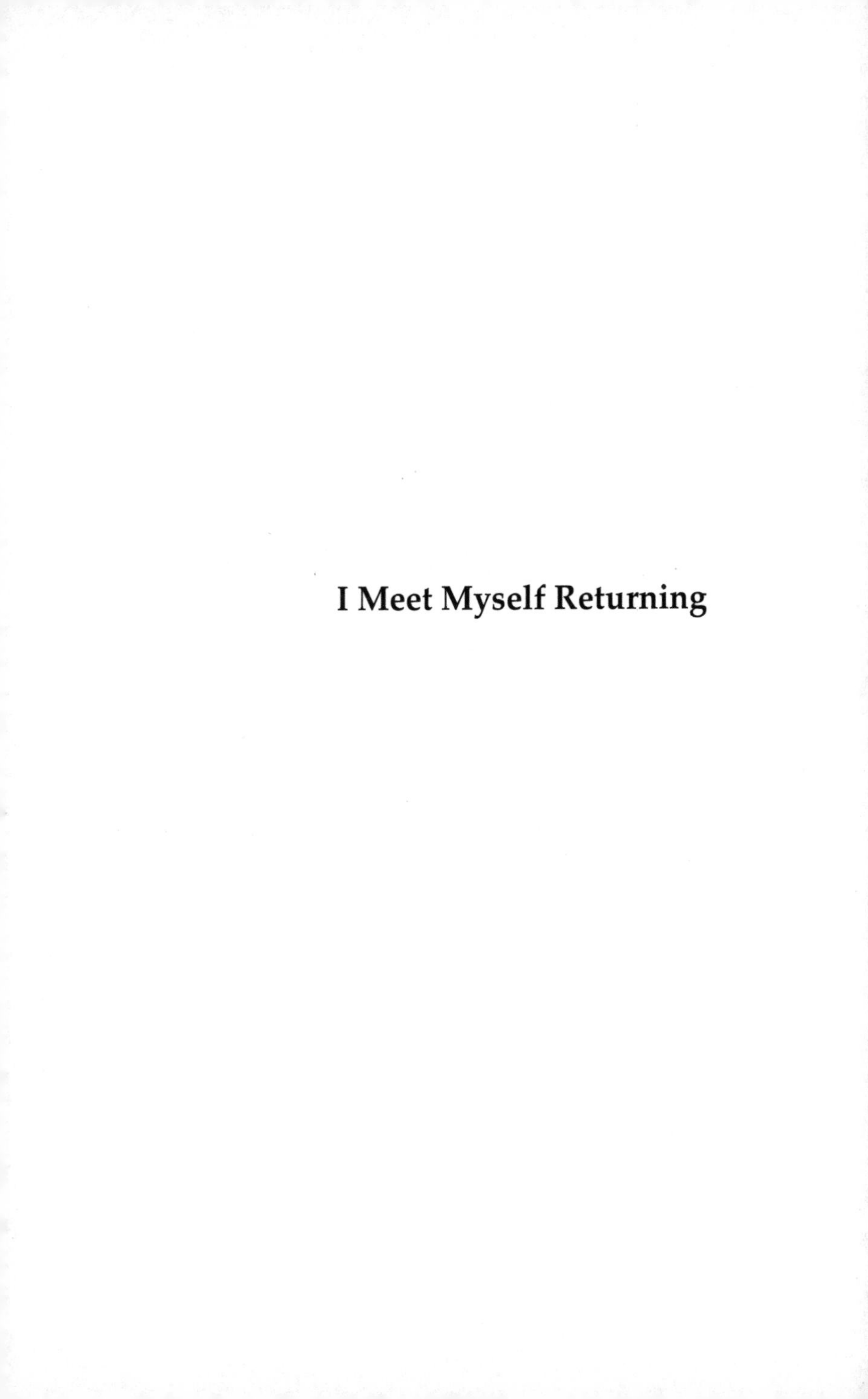

I Meet Myself Returning

Happy New Year

In the first eight hours of light we vow to abstain
for thirty nights.
This is clean-your-teeth easy,
we are not dipsos.

On the first night back from work
a twenty-years-together look.
The vacuum release of cork,
the clean waterfall rush of wine on glass.

In spring we keep in touch with friends.
Kids get in the way.
Pull our stomachs in,
laugh about summer fifteen years ago when we ran to fat.
Dim the mirror lights.

Escaping the chill pinch of autumn
we return from the east
debating potential heating bills.

We drink like oafs in December.

Pearl diving

Her knees like knotted cotton
ghost white hair rough-tousled
sun-pinched pinhole pupils
young girl parent-pleasing
wan and freckle-wristed
a seed of future beauty
avian-light
perching on the wall.

He stretches not to touch her
his longing now an art form
he whispers that it's killing
but it catches in the telling.
He makes a joke of 'masons
just to touch her cold hands
saves each petty message
waiting for the day
she says goodbye.

Her lips pressed to the cold cup
fingers curled and lissom
palms could blanch the bare flesh
as if the flesh would listen
as if her flesh would listen
as thirties turn to forties

lending a distraction.

Thinking of new ways to say goodbye.

Number 22

Nicotine drapes at 22,
film of dust on cup and plate,
Army Ron likes to masturbate
to the sound of neighbours fucking.

He left his mind in the Falklands.
When he took the keys he was on the up,
now it's four floors up and endless down.
The biscuit tin is plastic.

He keeps the treats in this plastic box
for the local kids who don't knock on –
a lack of trust in Army Ron
for his late hour shouts and screaming.

The stains on pants and one mile breath.
Mechanic's nails but he has no work.
Untouched treats in his biscuit box.
The grandkids never visit.

Nordic Hotel, Leeds 6

There was a student from Iran in the residents' lounge,
talked of bald heads and ponytails in the days pre-Ayatollah.

Two hundred miles from home
in a two-star guest house

with that weird spotted vinyl on the front of the bar.

The landlord wouldn't charge for soft drinks.
Must have thought we were poor.

At the owners' silver wedding
Dad claimed D-Day shrapnel stopped him from dancing.

He was twelve at the time of the landings.

Skipper

He calls the pilot *Skipper,*
a throwback to his Forces days,
searches under cushions
for imagined mislaid items
and the dark fog for something warm to clasp.

A picture of his grandson
takes pride of place at breakfast time,
stands in silence over
his tortuous morning ritual;
he's a clever fellow
flying solo at his age.

His pugilist-like body,
middleweight and rock-hewn tight,
formed from years of grafting;
now rapid in its fading,
a silhouette half-smudging in the haze.

When the fog is lifted,
for moments, minutes, half an hour
he mock grins at the mirror
then back at his companion
as if it's 1970
and whispers,
'Son, don't worry,
this may never happen.'

Thirteen Franciscans

For Marianne and Steve

Thirteen Franciscans created beauty from nothing
through love.

Love is not a crusade.

It is wet Wednesday in Whalley Range,
the twine of Rochdalian burr and Mancunian twang.

The giggling whisper of bed springs
gathering to love-laden laughter,
a head-shaking silent scream of joy.

A photograph
a painting
a poem.

His bristle of chinness
her ethereal slimness
their her and himness.
No glory to godness.

A hymnless song of praise.

And not a word of Spanish

Stretch-marked belly
sunbed glow
fake Givenchy head to toe
flying south where cheap wine flows
smoker's mouth, tattooed toes
heading where our own kind go
to colonise and prosper.

Inappropriate football shirts
obesity and bad breath flirts
leering at the local skirt
and not a word of Spanish.

We have Union Jacks for underwear
upside down but we don't care
we hate the Irish, Scots and Welsh
we're drunk on self-awareness.

The racists congregate in Spain
competing for the deepest tan
when we get home we know that Nan
is shovelling Diazepam.

Her progeny have failed the plan
we're darker than the darkies.

Stanley

He dances over Yorkshire
as an old man spreading dust
of angels on the mortal.

Takes pleasure from the movement
of limbs set free from worry,
creaking knees and clicking heels.

He used to graft in textiles
crafting heddle, shuttle, beam.
Now he tips his hat to strangers
and sways to his own tune.

The sadness of strangers just passing

Your umbrella hangs on the back of the seat,
the 17:30 to Crewe.
It is fringed with funny pink baubles
which dance to the rhythm of the track.

Your fingers were wrapped in the handles of bags
gifts for the kids, sisters and friends,
bruised and blushed by the twine round the tips,
shop tags removed as love has no price.

You may live in Levenshulme, Stockport or Crewe;
the gifts may end up unwanted.
No chatter, no smile, no kiss and no love,
the sadness of strangers just passing.

Strings

A heart has more strings
than you have taken.
I am plucking those now.

Play more tricks,
four strings or six.
I will counter-harmonise
in consecutive fifths.

The timpani of this
will be lost
on you.

Icicles

Footsteps slide in springtime snow,
the departing have to make a show
of leaving an impression.

The imprint of your booted feet
dismissed in fleeting fall of sleet
when Easter showers were frozen.

The dignity of letting go
destroyed by tracks of tears on snow
and icicles on nostrils.

Spring in Heywood

On the wall facing the flat
the hoarding changes weekly.
A grinning child selling supermarkets,
the snap of an amateur chef with a meal made glorious,
claims that phone connections are improving,
pictures of a distant paradise
expensive but apparently in reach.

Beneath the board
Ron's Cycles and Spares opens daily
without custom or passing interest.

The blacksmith in the unit to the side
opens at dawn but shoes no horses.
Occasionally knocks metal on metal
for unrecognisable purpose
to the rhythm of passing sirens.

A logo made of tyres designed in 1894
grins from Ron's shop front
delivering a vaguely Nazi salute.

Nunc est bibendum.

Football and girls

I long to be in a song by Simon and Garfunkel,
smoking, reading magazines on trains
in romantic isolation, dreaming of Anne Bancroft
as they harmonise on Widnes Station.

I long to be in sixties garb
with a mod-slim silhouette,
with the tone of Art Garfunkel,
an angel in a turtle-neck.

Speeding out of Sagana
in a steel-slick Greyhound bus
with the charm of young naïvety,
thinking Kennedy was at one with us.

Growing into man from boy
Cecilia played her part,
confirming universal truth
Only girls and football break your heart.

New school blues

January, as cold as sociopathy.
Stone flagged floors,
tiled polished walls
mulberry and filthy green,
elbow-greased to buggery.

The master stalks the corridors.
Oxford-brogued and ricket-legged
his trousers belted five meals tight,
inches from his previous waist.

He's married to misogyny
and swears in ancient Greek.

Melanie

Melanie at school had a swollen lip
from picking at the sore.
The first girl I kissed.

Her mother was from Bolton,
called me love when I knocked on,
left me feeling I was welcome.

She was never home.

Her imperfect mouth,
a hope still missed.
I fell on my arse
under the tree where we kissed.

He's whistling Sinatra

Hugh Bryn's brandy cork is popped;
much plumper than the tin-scrape sound,
the screw-top twist of cheaper brands,
bottles with no vintage.

Rockers, rappers it has sunk
from connoisseur to too much drunk,
no thrash or grunge in Hugh Bryn's room,
he's whistling Sinatra.

Mechanic's hands grip glass balloon,
quiver lips meet glass or tip,
the aroma of a slim cigar
or guilty cigarette.

Eccentric shake of cheek and jowls,
fingernails Swarfega clean
won't raise a glass to queen or priest,
seer or politician.

Ffynon Farm

There was a door at the foot of the stairs,
the feel of 1920s Wales and the stammer of the language.

1961 etched into the yard
looked the same in reverse.
Our home for two weeks; seemed like years.

Felicitous home with big-eared boys
and our parents' friends from Yorkshire.

There were hippies in the field,
amused us with their *yeah*s and *man*s,

a family from Urmston and rats by the cesspool,
we had no sense of time or plans.

Dad let me sit on his knee and pretend to drive
while dogs yapped at the wheels,
made that joke about Mr Mallett
crouching on the seat, changing gear in stutters.

Once we feigned a runaway,
hiding under hay bales with stolen food.
Waiting to be discovered.

The farmer pretended we were helping
while his sons swore at us in Welsh.

Mr Wilson said

My job was easy,
scavenging for scraps
under new machinery
all day.

The girls wore felted caps
to keep their hair in check,
sometimes it was ripped away
and with it they were gone.

On Sundays we had chapel
three times or more a day.
We had to read a verse
for the girls who'd gone away.

Twenty

Lost in the spider of streets
named after Dickens books,
I stopped to scrawp pockets.

Enough jangle
for a packet of three,
ten Embassy.
Balm for first-time nerves.

Up Pecksniff, down Dorrit.
Dombey Street eluded me.
November sweats
and expectation.

Vivaldi on the tape deck,
your home of Earl Grey tea
and patchouli.
A lanky architect
lurking in the kitchen.

You fucked me at five past three.

Palace of shyness

You meet me at the corner
and take me to the palace
where shyness takes us over.
Lend me a neurosis
or borrow one of mine.

Let me hear your footsteps
fall softly on the flora
to mingle with mine often,
and rarely stray too far from
or step too closely in them.

Unearth some buried ego.
Add opiate of presence
but never dig so deep
to find the cruelty within us.

Lend me a neurosis
or borrow one of mine.

The transparent truth of Scientology

I accept the applause
for embracing the penis enhancement drugs
before you.

I expect you to accept
that the poetry prize was withdrawn
through tacit refusal.

I reject the notion
that I'm a misery
for non-attendance
at the old boys' reunion.

I wonder why
I never found God
despite the transparent truth
of Scientology.

I am lachrymose to know
that I have six
unattributed kids

all of whom hate me and
howl every night
that the penis enhancement
worked.

At four o'clock

At four o'clock depression lifts,
a grand relief from workday shifts
of mundane tasks to pay the bills
to hold off drink and popping pills.
Three cheers for these unwanted gifts,

bad hangovers and workday rifts
are food to feed a mind that drifts
to dreams of beaches, snow-capped hills,
at four o'clock.

The office worker's time to sift
old love affairs, the ones that drift
from heart half-stopped to making wills
to knitting scarves for winter chills
and saving up for staircase lifts,
at four o'clock.

Fifty-five winters

Hair, lost by nature or desire
defines a body
puffed by pastry, drink and occasional torpor.
The half-inflated rubber ring of
a prosperous pork butcher.

Hands, light-fingered in
youth with cigarettes and toffees
that tended a sick father
and girls of scant attention,
now occupied with holding on
and frequent masturbation.

September

Nestled snug
between two breasts of hills
the crabber's grave is tranquilised by distance
and my happy pills.

I spent all summer working,
sorting corn ears from the chaff,
awaiting your awakening,
your tickled-pink half-belly laugh,
your shades of independence,
your poor drinking capacity
compared to hardened lushes.

I crush a dimp between my thumb
and my calloused gnarled forefinger

and think if we were young and free
that each fold and crease of your skin
is impression made by mine
and no-one else's.

You nose your head into a book
and toss your ghostly mane,
borderline leonine,
bespectacled and pondering.

I curse the laws of nature
that force river-flow one way.
Your blood courses likewise,
by gravity or tide,

in that picture of felicity;
you two grinning, side by side.

In a water-sun September,
in heat-stretched skin and bone,
you gaze from book to crabber's grave.
Your look says
we're born and die alone.

Islands

My Father found green fingers in his fifties
How we mocked his passage into middle age;
with the naïvety of the colour, no envy.
The lawn sprung emerald under his touch.

We sat with brandy
and stuttered friendship in his field of greens.
I touched on my desire to free Ireland.
'As a haughty outsider,' he scoffed.

Where there's a will

The gate you didn't hang too well
on the patch you didn't tend too well
and the mind you didn't take to
I have walked through.

The woods behind the houses
where building wasn't planned too well
that sit in this dark valley, well,
the trees are there to take me.

The friends I didn't know too well
or had no time to know me, well,
I'll say goodbye if they can tell
in whispers.

The man you talked about so well
who didn't cope with much too well
was hanging by a thread too long,
now dangles on the twine.

Carp fishing in Shropshire

I could go carp fishing in Shropshire.
Pitch a tent with a quart of spirits,
fish through the night
taking occasional sips
and a gulp with each bite.

I could walk five miles to town,
stroll from book shop to library,
taking in architecture,
supping water to stop night cramps
with a late small tincture for sleep.

I could remedy lost education,
learn Welsh as a family nod,
wander far and wide
chatting aimlessly to shopkeepers
and passers-by.

I will go to the pub too often,
repeat myself to irritated bar staff.
Fart prolifically without knowing,
forget who I am
and die.

Seven hills

I don't recall what made us laugh like giants.
Two days into the trip,
freedom from partners to stop our morning drinking
loosened us like infants.

We hooted into our glasses,
revelled in the echo
as children in a cave.

On the bridge
a scamp relieved you of your cards and wallet.
Your appreciation of the child thief's skill defines you.

We shared beers with the cash that was left,
that quiet bar in Ortaköy
with the feel of Sunday night at home.

The staff used a four foot door
to stoop into the bar,
you wouldn't believe me at first.

You took that picture of me
gurning through it while the barman was away.

The tissue seller

There's a Starbucks by the new bridge now,
in the place where a merchant used to live
or the school house was
or the walls were home to a famous local writer.

The mosque is in repair again,
prayer calls find indifferent ears,
the locals line the Starbucks' walls
in relaxed sophistication.

A scruffy lad with twisted limbs
sells tissues for a few kuruş,
his Turkish barely audible
through his malformed lips and manner.

Bana yardım et, bana yardım et, he mumbles,
but he can't be heard.

Bana yardım et, bana yardım et, *please help me,*
but we didn't.

Headscarves glide past unclothed limbs,
winter coats past dancing folk
and charity begins at home
is our altruistic mantra.

Syrian bombs bomb Syrian kids
six hundred miles or a world away,
but no one here will raise a lid
to pay a lira for ten tissues.

After Orhan Veli Kanık

We would have drunk and
smoked,
told dirty jokes.
Loved the same women,
seldom cleaned our teeth.

Ate leblebi in dirty bars,
turned those rags into these stars
that we gawp in Gülhane Park.
Monday morning early,
jobless drunk and worthy.

Death by drunken fall

Edna St Vincent Millay
my spirit is broken today,
come with me down to the Galata Bridge
where the country kids fish
and their prey is the tourist.

The expanse of the Bosphorus waters
like an ocean of drink lies before us.
We can start after breakfast with gin infused tea
eat leblebi with rakı in the Kemalist way,
we can stroll down to Bebek where the rich locals play
and do things we might be ashamed of.

On the ferry to old Kadıköy
Orhan travelled this way man and boy;
you need to converse with this town's favourite bard,
your desire for hard drinking
coincides with his thinking,
I know that you won't disappoint.

Seabirds scream their song to the nation
overhead in strange murmuration,
wild wind whips the water to dwarf-dancing surf,
an old man drinks tea through a whole sugar lump
and lights one cigarette from another.

In the bar at the Bebek hotel
where folk hide their loneliness well,
like any town's bar where the smoke fug and glow
hides our cares from ourselves,
we'll pretend we don't know.
They'll return like a ghost in the morning.

Dawn in Galata

Seagulls squawk as if to mock us
trudging up bleak hills to work,
for the drudgery we suffer
that they don't find on the wing.

The Ezan cry at 5 o'clock
fleetingly drowns out their cries;
they don't answer calls to prayer,
they've no conscience or regret.

There is no love or jealousy,
no pitied poor or wealthy,
no avian symposia
to dictate what's right and wrong.

We barely notice darkness fall
as hands turn from lathe to glass
and drink to life's futility
with our old meyhane songs.

All we are is love and death,
desire and wistful transience,
casual ephemera
and tiresome peccadillos.

Every soul is on the scale
from vacant gaze to knowing nod,
not knowing where the lonely stops
and even less the longing.

Cheap wine and pills and pointless lists,
heaving guts heave gutlessness,
as you kneel above him in the night
there's no pleasure in the knowing.

The scent of you half floating past,
the shape of you perambulates.
The you of you just being
has me rattling and shaking.

Balm

Twenty winters on
in the twilight of your autumn,
barefoot and silhouetted
pot stirring at the stove.
Your high backside not withered
or worn by years' time passing,
unchanged by love or longing,
a grandchild at your hip.

You turn in animation
to show your face is wracked by tracks
from tears of separation;
then swivel and return
to chopping up the onion.

Rascal

I bow my smokestack slowly,
like a rascal steal under the bridge.
I've had Imam's backsides on my benches,
Ottoman Princes lay makeshift beds
to rest their heads in my hull,

I've seen fire sweep the hills unabated,
make smokestacks taller than mine.
I've seen men look like Hell
as they bob on the swell
from the Bosphorus out to the brine,

I have been the witness of whispers and trysts,
seen classes of men set apart by loose lips.
I've seen tears shed at dawn
as men left their first born
for the Crescent, the Star and the Sword,

pickpockets pick pockets on the bridge overhead
while lovers find fame in their books.
I've seen young turn to old in the blink of an eye,
faces grow cold from wars and lost love

and I wonder how long I will linger
to see the cycle of life turn again.
My bones left to rot in the breaker's yard,
yours flake to dust in the field on the hill
in time long forgotten like mine.

Manchester, my winter

Mascara smudge and pillow shaped
by head now gone and back to home
where paying bills and being straight
and tying gifts with fingertips
that did a trick for me last night
is how it has to be.

He won't know and she won't know
but we know where this thing will go –
where rivers wide and thoughts ill-shaped
by time's raw fate
and love and hate
meet cul-de-sacs of nothing.

The scent of hair and hair on clothes,
make-up flaked on last night's threads,
threads of lives and beads of sweat –
we haven't seen betrayal yet –
accelerate the fire

from flush of youth to long time dead,
twelve years in someone else's bed,
you bring yourself to hold my gaze.
Dilation gives the game away.
Your omnipresent verbal pause
accented pure Mancunian,
the tremor of your shyness.

In taxi queues at five past three
where office workers take their drink

like once-teetotal pledge-takers –
Methodism in their madness.
You lean right in, hips sway away
and take a cab the wrong way, south.
I often dream but seldom sleep,
the vacuum of your absence.

Dreich

The darkest dreich of dankest hills,
the misery of disused mills,
the pouting lips of windowsills,
frames unglazed for decades.

No one knows, no one cares.
Your eyes reflect the hole within.
The blankest stare, black eyes are pinned
to something we can't measure.

The mill towns look attractive now
to fifty-somethings looking for
escape from fights and spoiled face kids,
the black hole is remaining.

Dreich as fuck, horizontal rain,
no reception on the phone.
Solitude won't dull the pain
of love and disappointment.

I meet myself returning

The screen door slams on Thunder Road.
I emerge from the ginnel at the top of the street,
fake the motion of a screen swinging shut,
instantly embarrassed.

The pram girl, flushed with shame for my moves,
drops jaw to floor when 'Mary's dress waves'
croaks from my mouth implausibly,
failed singer's dream apparent.

There's a house that clings to Heathbank Road,
the family has long escaped,
left mother to her mutterings,
no intention of a visit.

The west coast line procrastinates,
creeping into Cheadle Hulme
alive with happy travellers,
less happy, if they're human.

The loop I walk at four mile pace
past posh boys' schools and rambling men.
Whichever way I take
I meet myself returning.

The ale glass

A four mile stretch of calf and thigh
exaggerated swing of arms
to reach the Inn for six
to build a thirst to slake.

The hop crop is perennial
to service rows of sand-dry mouths
of those that hope there's more in time
than fatherhood and duty.

The urgent rush of acorn flow
drawn from pump by tattooed arm
fills the glass with bitter clouds
before lips meet to taste.

Trick of toffee, hoppy nose
trickles down to empty guts
arthritic fingers keep the grip
of lance-straight glass with brewer's mark
of tiger, otter, rose.

The landlord turns the jukebox down
a volume indiscernible
to ears drummed out by factory sounds
and domestic complications.

Four gulps in the head subsides
patterns form for drunks' debate
super-clustered galaxies
dubious Picasso prints
elongated continents
the face of Jesus Christ.

Listening to Sinatra

Bibliophiles cannot get to the library
for leaves on the line,
friends left behind
or similar excuses.

Reading is calming.
Time is short for drinking and bumbling
from one disaster to the next.
Men never learn.
Elephants never forget.

Listening to Sinatra
is catharsis in reverse.
Imagining the '50s never happened
or we are different to our parents.

When we get there
we don't know what to read.

It's opening time.